For Phyllis Lee,

A great voice!

Sincerely,
Joseph McLaughlin
OPD 2003

Joseph McLaughlin

GREATEST HITS
1970-2000

Joseph McLaughlin $8.95
GREATEST HITS 1970-2000
Greatest Hits Series #74   ISBN 1-930755-92-9

Copyright 2001 Joseph McLaughlin
All rights reserved. Pudding House retains permission to reprint.
To copy/print any of these poems individually, permission must first be obtained from the author in writing.
FIRST EDITION
Printed in the United States of America

Pudding House Publications
60 North Main Street
Johnstown Ohio 43031
740-967-6060   pudding@johnstown.net   www.puddinghouse.com

ACKNOWLEDGMENTS

We thank the editors of the following publications where poems first appeared:

"3 Apples," *Xanadu*
"Cupid," *Journal of Contemporary Poets*
"Into the Realm of Signs," *The Green Horse for Poetry*
"James Davis, Trumpeter," *Southern Poetry Review*
"Kassiopeia," *Ab Intra*
"Kodak: Dream Frames," *The Free Lance*
"La Mer," *The Green Horse for Poetry*
"Litany at 2 a.m.," *Big Moon*
"Pale Horses," *Confrontation*
"To Ann at the Summer Solstice," *The Green Horse for Poetry*

Publisher's Position Statement on the Value of Poetry Arts

This chapbook is limited edition fine art from the poet

Joseph McLaughlin

whose work you support for a few cents per page. You are not buying paper and printer's ink by weight. You selected language art that took as long to create as paintings or other fine art. Pudding House caters to those who understand the value of the poet's good work. We are in business to make and enhance reputations rather than to assure profits for our press. Poets are chosen on the basis of their contribution to literary arts and to the popular culture. On behalf of a large community of contemporary poets, this poet in particular, independent and small press publishing, and Pudding House Publications, thank you for your patronage.

Joseph McLaughlin
GREATEST HITS
1970-2000

Contents

Introduction 5

Cupid 11
Into the Realm of Signs 12
James Davis, Trumpeter 13
Kassiopeia 14
Kodak: Dream Frames 15
La Mer 16
Litany at 2 A.M. 17
Pale Horses 18
Paneling My Daughter's Room 19
3 Apples 20
To a Ballerina 21
To Ann at the Summer Solstice 22

INTRODUCTION

My earliest profound experience with poetry came in the two-room annex to St. Joseph's grade school in Canton, Ohio. One winter afternoon in the sixth grade I encountered Emily Dickinson's "A fly buzzed when I died," and everything changed for me. The little poem was so very different from the traditional poems we'd been reading; it seemed modern and innovative--and challenging in the way it contrasted a trivial event with one's death. I felt as if I'd momentarily visited an unusual new world.

I say "momentarily" since I didn't think very much about poetry for the next few years, although I listened very carefully to song lyrics as the era of rock 'n roll was just beginning. I graduated in 1958 from Timken High School in Canton where the closest I came to poetry or poets was the requirement to read Carl Sandburg's biography of Lincoln.

However, in my freshman English class at Ohio State the next winter quarter, I was assigned to go hear Robert Frost who would be on campus. When the big day came, the auditorium was full for what I came to realize was a major event. I was mesmerized by this rough-hewn, white-haired man in gray clothes who so resembled his name. One man on stage, reading his poems and commenting with wry wisdom on his place in the universe: this was my first encounter with a major cultural icon, and I was so taken by the experience that I completely forgot to do the report which was required. I found myself later trying to convince the professor that I really had attended the program. "That's OK. I'll give you a B in the course," he said with an understanding smile. (That was also my first experience with grades by negotiation, but that's another topic!)

The Frost encounter let me know that poets could possibly be alive and that poetry need not be a province for only women and homosexuals! Still, I did little with the topic after the memory of the reading faded. In those days, I was determined to become--of all things--a golf professional and eventually did so for about a year and a half, during which I worked at two different clubs and played no golf as the members required my attention from dawn to dusk. In order to earn a real living (there was little money in golf in those days) I eventually found work in the bearing factory at the Timken Company which enabled my new wife and our growing family to live in unaccustomed splendor: At the wage of $2.35 an hour, I was able to pay off my debts and buy a car and a house!

And I found time to begin reading again. As a child I'd haunted the library and was regularly run out of the adult (meaning "not juvenile") sections until the librarians realized I was reading at that level. Perhaps inspired by his role at the inauguration of John F. Kennedy, I actually began to *read* the poems of Robert Frost—backwards. I started with his last book, "In the Clearing," and decided I, too could write poems. As bad as they were, those early attempts at self-expression had some quality; but after being embarrassed by my first publication in the local newspaper, I realized I had much to learn about this "craft and sullen art." Two years later, at 26, I earned my first "real" publication in *Spirit*, the magazine of The Catholic Poetry Society.

Over the next ten or twelve years, I became consumed with acquiring an education and moving through the Timken Company's factories into—of all places—the mechanical engineering department. All the while I was reading, writing, and publishing not only poems, but stories and articles for popular magazines such as *Stock Car Racing* and *Mother Earth News*. I saw myself as a writer who had to work at something. I directed the Midwest Writers Conference at Malone College in the 1970's, and took personally the challenge of guest speaker Hayes Jacobs that "a writer—a real writer—can write anything." At work, I was engaged in a great deal of technical writing; and our family was into motorcycles, boats, camping, auto racing, and jogging. I subscribed to Philip Roth's premise that "nothing really bad can happen to a writer—it's all material." Facing all the problems of getting published which every writer deals with, I founded Pale Horse Press in 1974, issuing three annual anthologies along with the poems of Walter Griffin and Lyle Crist over the next several years.

At the age of 38, and with four children in our home, I blithely took a fifty percent pay cut and entered education. I taught two years at the local parochial high school after realizing on the first day that this was the wrong age group for me to work with! Eventually, I was recruited to join the faculty at Stark Technical College in 1980, where my industrial background and liberal arts education combined for a perfect fit for the next twenty years. The only disenchantment I experienced was the realization that this was no ivory tower. The load of teaching both day and evening classes and the continual burden of grading made it very difficult to continue writing and publishing. In fact, one of many collapsed escape tunnels I began to construct was a five-year diversion into public relations, advertising, and marketing, mainly for motorsports events. It was a great education, and the business issues gave me lots of material for the business communication and technical writing courses I taught every term. But I didn't write or place many poems during that era. To the contrary, I issued thousands of press releases to local and trade papers and found myself being as scrupulous as a poet to avoid repeating a word in the same release! Realizing the value of space in commercial magazines and newspapers is great training for a writer. (Think of Hemingway and Thurber.)

     All the while, I was a full time professor who completed a book, *High School Cross Country*, for Track & Field News Press during his master's degree year (1983). Along the way I kept Pale Horse Press going, focusing now on my own books. My golf experience led to *Zen in the Art of Golf*, a collection of brief essays which has been in print for over 10 years. I also used the text in a continuing education course called Enjoy Golf! A companion novella, *Golf is the Devil's Game*, appeared in 1997. My current collection of poems is *Memory, In Your Country*, which was issued in 1995. Finally, a bit worn from it all, I retired from the college in May 2000 at the age of 59, released to be what everyone dreams of becoming: a full time writer!

     When I began to review poems for this Greatest Hits collection, I thought the choices would be easy. Then I had several sobering realizations. I began this work when I was 24. Now I am 60. That meant evaluating 36 years of writing and publishing activity! It was also a surprise to discover that—perhaps like an athlete—my best work may have been done in the early years. Certainly, I had some significant publications in the 1970's and '80's. And those poems had all my requirements: a vivid image, contemporary language, and a moment of intensity. I relied upon them for many years at readings until one day I realized I may be repeating myself before audiences. *That* got me started writing again!

I printed out 25 or so poems from which to choose, then asked myself: What should be the criteria for selecting just 12? My ego favored those that appeared in prestigious publications, such as *Hiram Poetry Review*, *Southern Poetry Review*, and *Field*. But I also felt each *Greatest Hit* should be substantial in its own right, and memorable in that it was requested at readings. Finally, I wanted to pick those which I enjoyed reading the most At last (or alas) here they are!.

As the reader makes his way through this little collection, he will notice a number of classical allusions, for it is my belief that a spark of divinity powers each of us, and that the attributes of various deities--Greek, Roman, and Hebrew—are discernible in each individual. It may be helpful to have copies of Edith Hamilton's *The Greek Way* and *The Roman Way* handy along with *Bulfinch's Mythology*. The reading will be a richer experience—and who else is keeping this stuff alive? My greatest compliment was a rejection with a handwritten note: "Too mythic and legendary." Yes!

I might add that being selected for lifetime achievement awards or "best of" collections tends to suggest that one is near the end of it all. Conversely, I am writing more than ever (retirement allows that) and experimenting with new material, style, and forms. Is there hope for a *Greatest Hits II*? Enjoy— and stay tuned!

—Joseph McLaughlin
New Philadelphia, Ohio
May 2001

The Poems

CUPID

Cupid, reduced to a babe on greeting cards,
once startled Psyche with his beauty
when she, ignoring his prudent warning,
dared cast a lamp upon his sleeping form.

Angered by her faithlessness,
he slept on park benches
or worked old steamers in the China Sea,
romantic as Conrad's Jim.
                                        But he
has remembered the darkened temple, the couch
where his touch was a light in the darkness.

Now the girls laugh fondly at his feathers;
maternally they view the cherub lip,
unaware that he still slings his arrows
and that Love's poison smiles upon each tip.

INTO THE REALM OF SIGNS

Poet, writer—I am wary of the label
if he is a lisping boy
in lavender sleeves
placing scented petals
on your staring eyes;

if she is a well-rouged grandmother
with blue-tinted hair
pressing her soft thighs around
a photograph of Rod McKuen;

if he is unintelligible,
the words tangled in his dirty hair;
he runs his fingers through it,
dropping on us
syllables and dandruff.

There must be another name
for this communicant;
another name for his descent
into the realm of signs
where some of the words are altar breads
and some of them are wines.

JAMES DAVIS, TRUMPETER

It is a style he has, of satyr
or cool man in his element
when, between rasping phrases of his song,
he flips the microphone from hand to hand—
the hot, living connection with the bodies
hidden in the darkness.
                                  Around the stage
faces ride in the green light of table candles,
flickering, come from a lost world to sit
drunken and cheering in the hall of music.

He has the stance of a clarion, blowing sweet or wild
over the terraces of Jerusalem, *Taps* for the Union dead,
a cavalry charge.

Big Jim plays three horns at once, thrusting
the instruments into the intervals of sound,
parrying the air with *riposte, en garde*!

and the glistening bells
of the trumpet, cornet, and valve trombone
shimmer in the gale of one man's breath
as Jimmy moves in the blue world
with fists of gleaming brass.

KASSIOPEIA

Your dawn-gray eyes have followed me
across the Alleghenies
to Syracuse and Baltimore

and now, in Philadelphia,
I traverse the heavy drapes at six
to encounter, at the thermopane, your face.

Your smile is vague today—
of mist and fog the sun can't burn
in the cold furnace of November.

Like one of Whistler's last abstractions,
you come to lead me deeper into winter
knowing I am already lost.

But promise just a small fire
on the mountain where the glacier rises,
a hot brandy in the cavern's mouth,

an instrument to pluck,
and I will even learn to praise
your cold, white hands at my throat.

KODAK: DREAM FRAMES

In the same recurring dream
you appear
in a Japanese garden, the willows
and the seasons and your dress
changing like slides, at random—

from brocaded silk to summer cotton
to wool that rivals the whiteness
of the snowy ground.
                    Your hair
drawn back or hanging loose
like a dark wing,

you walk through the changing frames
and the green leaves of the trees
go brown, vanish, then are green again.

Small flames flower in your footsteps.
Once you lift your hand
in some ineffable gesture.

Each night you burn clean paths
across the dense, dreaming screen.
Your eyes

trace my intimate, blue veins
filling me with the luck of words.

LA MER

I have not sailed your green, Pacific swells,
weedy Sargasso doldrums,
nor haunted regions
of the wine-dark Aegean.

There are latitudes of yours
I cannot reach, fabled islands
below the *Horse* and *Roaring 40's*;
but I have heard that wind
from screaming round the Horn,
diminish to an urgent whisper.

I have never seen
your bronze, evening eyes
light the Indian ocean
like a sun carried on its shield,
the clarity of the Caribbean
give up to storm.

Those are the charming lies
of other, braver mariners.
I only know the crisp
chop of an Atlantic
eating at the beaches,

the way your waters,
furrowed by my prow,
are smoothly spread
until you fold the foaming wake
around my transom
with blue, smiling hands.

LITANY AT 2 A.M.

I do not grieve for the dead,
still in their palace rooms and vaults;
not even for the lost, the unknown
soldiers and drowned fishermen
who go to earth and water
unmarked by stone.

Nor do I grieve for the recent births
of infants, their blue-veined skulls
poised above the font
for the oil and salt
and splash of christening.

It is not for you nor any woman
that I weep,
salt from the darkness
becoming a promise on the lips
telling of my time and futile deeds,

but for my rumpled life
and awkward majesty
and for the mortal drumbeat of this heart
resounding
in the ruined abbey of sleep.

PALE HORSES

Carrying their burden of dreams,
white horses clatter
down the steep paths
toward the mercury-vapor lights
and empty highways
of the sleeping city.

Like figures stampeding from a myth
they emerge
in unlikely neighborhoods and disperse
gently whinnying on the common streets
and garden walks, leaping
to the low apartment balconies,
the sagging, back-porch roofs.

Long heads peer into windows.
Soft muzzles nose your children
until they cry out in sleep, strangely
taken, warmly soiling the beds
in rare occasion.

Before you can answer each cry,
the horses have vanished:
                        Dim
stampings and snortings
splintering the sill of youth;
                        pale images
flashing into years of myth.

In the corridor amid the screams,
dressed in a cold night sweat,
you cannot recall exactly
when you last were frightened
by a white mare's visit.

PANELING MY DAUGHTER'S ROOM

I promised to do this
before she leaves for college
or to be married.

Power tools and scraps
cover the floor,
and I step carefully,
fearing to kick a sabre-saw
rattling into action
around my ankles.

I am spending the day indoors
constructing this dormer
for a princess
while the yellow light
swirls outside the windows.

I must hurry. I must finish
before the tall, green knight arrives.
Even now he camps on the autumn highways
fueling a chromiumed, chopped Harley

while the serpents of my own summer
lie coiled amid the orange and yellow
cords of Black & Decker tools,
waiting to strike my naked heel.

Even now, like the uncle of Heloise,
I wish I could hide her
amid the lilies and stone of the convent.

3 APPLES

All week my wife has packed
apples in my lunch.
                    I have them
on a tray in my desk, arranged
in a row like polished
trophies of the noon hour,
or shrunken heads,
or the small, red hearts
of stuffed animals, the bears
and lions our children love.

Or maybe they are poison,
gifts to Snow White
from the mirror's face;
or maybe they are the promises loosed
when Eve uncrossed her knees.

I use them like an abacus
to count the week.
Two more days and I am free.

You understand.
I am not eating apples.

TO A BALLERINA

In the profile of your face, one line
from the forehead to the tip of the nose;
and when you turn like a small flamingo
ankle-deep in water, neck arched,
I see the serenity of the nun's expression
muting the delicate passion of your feathers.

Child-woman, bird poised for flight,
your voice is a melody heard through many veils,
a far-off carousel, dull and dear.
Yet, to what music do you move?
Some inner sound must lead you like a rhyme
down these spiral stairs of Time:

for, even as you walk, a bell
forms in the light around you,
its clapper gently striking with your hips
as you carefully point each foot,
perfectly controlling
your limbs, your heart, your lips.

TO ANN AT THE SUMMER SOLSTICE
In the distance the birches are like columns of silver.
—Blaise Cendrars

Driving home from the lake last night, the moon rose perfectly over the fields. Everyone in the car was sleeping, but I described aloud all the barns we passed, imagining they were filled with wide-awake animals, restless in rough stalls, striped like zebras from the light slicing through cracked and gaping boards.

I told your sleeping ear about the big, old houses covered with aluminum siding that creaked in the moonlight; how the television towers were guyed to old, brick chimneys. Farmers and their plump wives were asleep in upper rooms; you could almost hear the whir of the air-conditioners as we sailed past.

These are the towns that lie south of Erie: Norwalk, Ashland, Wooster, New Pittsburg, Applecreek, Beach City, Strasburg, Dover. Somewhere, nearby, there is a real *Winesburg, Ohio*.

Ann, I said, they lie along the road like gates, admitting us deeper and deeper into the state. The white signs flared in the head lamps as we crossed their borders. You stirred on my shoulder and I looked at my watch.

On a night just like this, after twenty years, Odysseus came strolling home across the moonlit fields, dressed like a beggar, to pet the dying Argus, bend the impossible bow, shoot the arrow through 12 axeheads, slay the suitors, and bed at last, again and again, a Penelope anxious as you.